The Sustainable Living Book for Beginners:

A Self-Sufficiency Starter

Or

How To Be a Self Reliant Homesteader
& Have a Simple Life, Living Off Grid

Frank Randall

@BackyardFarmBks
facebook.com/BackyardFarmBooks
backyardfarmbooks.com

Copyright © 2013 Frank Randall & 3D4T

All rights reserved.

This book contains material protected under International and Federal Copyright laws and Treaties. Any unauthorized reprint or use of this material is prohibited.

Unauthorized duplication or distribution of this material in any form is strictly prohibited. Violators will be prosecuted to the fullest extent of the law.

No part of this publication may be reproduced, stored in a retrieval system or transmitted in any form or by any means, electronic, mechanical, photocopying, recording or otherwise, without prior written permission from the author/publisher.

The author, publisher, and distributor of this product assume no responsibility for the use or misuse of this product, or for any physical or mental injury, damage and/or financial loss sustained to persons or property as a result of using this system. The liability, negligence, use, misuse or abuse of the operation of any methods, strategies, instructions or ideas contained in the material herein is the sole responsibility of the reader.

The material contained in this publication is provided for information purposes only.

ISBN: 1482610469
ISBN-13: 978-1482610468

DEDICATION

To backyard owners everywhere -
whether a farmer in your heart or just your dreams.

CONTENTS

Introduction	vii
1 - What Is Sustainable Living?	9
2 - Improving Your Life By Improving The Planet	11
3 - Growing Your Own Food	15
4 - What If Gardening Isn't For Me?	23
5 - Keeping Your Own Livestock	25
6 - Energy Sources and Consumption	33
7 - Sustaining The Earth By Managing Waste	45
8 - Getting Kids Involved with Your New Lifestyle	57
9 - 22 of the Biggest Lifestyle Tips	61
10 - Set a Goal and Make Your Plan	63
Conclusion	67
Shopping List	69
About the Author	71
Your Free Gift	73
Also From This Author	75

INTRODUCTION

If you've spent any time watching the TV news lately, chances are you've seen at least one piece about the environment—and how our lifestyle has torn it apart over the last 100 years.

It's hard to imagine describing modern life without using the words "green" and "environment." Most scientists consider our planet under threat, and as various media outlets continue to proclaim, it is up to us to do something about it.

However, many of us don't know what to do. We feel hopelessly lost when it comes to strategies and methods that will enable us to look after our planet. In fact, many of us feel that our existence actively harms our world on a daily basis.

Relax. You're not killing the planet. And the good news is that living sustainably, in a way that helps protect the environment, is not an unattainable dream. If you proceed slowly and carefully, you can make small changes here and there that will push you towards a life of true sustainability.

Since moving from the hustle and bustle of a metropolitan Northern England city to the peaceful shores of Lake Erie, I have had more space and time to experiment with various methods of sustainability and self-sufficiency. In this book, I will share the simplest, most effective and straightforward ways you can make a lasting difference for your home, family and environment.

All the very best,

Frank

Frank Randall

1

WHAT IS SUSTAINABLE LIVING?

It's more than just doing certain things at certain times. It's not a checklist or a tip sheet. It is a way of life. To live in a sustainable fashion, you need to be concerned with a number of issues including:

- Leaving something behind for future generations
- Reducing the cost of living
- Humane treatment of animals
- Ridding the planet of landfills
- Having next to no negative impact upon the environment

Okay, we know that modern life makes it difficult to have "no impact" upon the environment. But it is possible to hit that next to no impact target. Getting all of this right and locked into our way of living doesn't mean that we can't enjoy the process. We must leave a legacy, but we can also help to make the world a better place to live in today.

Consider these other ways in which sustainable living can help you and the planet:

Better health

Practicing sustainable living principles will make you healthier by reducing nasty toxins in your system.

Growing your own food

Growing your own food, including raising your own livestock, is a sensible choice when living sustainably. We'll talk about this more later.

Getting rid of waste

We mentioned landfills earlier. Embracing sustainable living requires you to avoid their use whenever possible, becoming a master of recycling. Reducing waste includes energy consumption as well—something we'll look at a bit later.

Ditching harmful chemicals

It is all too easy to disregard the chemicals in our household products. Often they are harmful to the environment and our families. Sustainable living will remove many harmful chemicals from your life.

Getting started and staying the path

There's a lot to take in over the next few chapters, but the ultimate goal is achievable. You just need to commit to making one small step at a time.

2

IMPROVING YOUR LIFE BY IMPROVING THE PLANET

We will start by looking at some of the basics of sustainability. Once you have an understanding of the fundamental principles, you'll soon feel ready to begin making the small changes that will eventually improve your world.

Technology progresses at such a rate that we often struggle to get a handle on how it works. It is making the world feel smaller while also making it a place where things can happen very fast.

Farming has changed. The machine has replaced the horse and cart. This means that things happen faster and more efficiently. Unfortunately, the agricultural industry uses large quantities of fossil fuels just to make sure that the farming takes place at the right levels. And when it comes to the end result of that crop—the food itself—it's modified (often genetically), mass produced, and jetted around the world on airplanes. A problem? Yes, very much so.

Chemicals

As recently as a few decades ago, most household cleaning products contained just a fraction of the chemical ingredients you find in them today. These products were simpler, relying more upon the hard work of the person doing the cleaning than the chemicals inside. These days, things are different. We want rapid results with as little effort as possible. These additional chemicals are often extremely toxic to wildlife and the environment. More often than not, they end up going down our drains or into the air and the ground, polluting the environment terribly. However, if you live sustainably, this does not have to happen.

Good news for the pocket

If you do so correctly, making the change to a sustainable lifestyle is not costly—it can actually save you money. Growing your own food, for example, is a great way to be frugal while providing your family with delicious and healthy protein and produce. Living sustainably means that you find ways to cut down on many things including spending.

Good news for the soul

Most of us are not bad people. We really want the very best for our children and the environment. Switching to a sustainable lifestyle will deliver just that. These practices really can help shape the future of our planet.

While we are on the topic of legacy, think about the terrible state of consumerism in which we live. Too many of us were brought up to feel that "more is more," and the sad fact is that we tend to think that the more we own, the better off we are. This is not true. Part of our legacy should be to change the mindset that suggests we need to be excessive. It is time to lead a much simpler life. This means thinking intelligently about what we have and why we should be grateful for it. Living to meet our actual needs, rather than the perceived needs that the media have suggested for us, means that we can gain some inner peace, too.

Take a deep breath

Think about it. If you are reducing waste and leaving less of an imprint on the world, you will be making the air quality better—or at least more bearable. This is important, as there are an ever-increasing number of allergies affecting the young as well as the old. If we want to ensure that our world literally becomes a cleaner place to live, we can make a huge difference by living cleaner. Take the simple act of planting a tree. This activity is possible for all of us, even if we don't own a garden. There are plenty of associations and societies that will help us to do so—cleaning the air and improving it for everybody as a result.

Spread the habit

When we do something good, we improve the chances that someone will copy us. Planting a tree is a great example. If we tell our friends that we have done this, they may consider planting a tree as well. This leads to a kind of chain reaction with people mimicking our activities and then telling someone they know—who goes on to copy them and tell the next person.

Just one person making a small change can start a domino effect on the attitudes of their family, friends and colleagues, spreading sustainability like a virus!

Frank Randall

3

GROWING YOUR OWN FOOD

We live in a world where growing your own food is no longer the norm—and to many, it can actually seem quite bizarre. This is because food is so readily available in the Western world. At any time of the day or night, at any time of year, all you have to do is get up and go down the street to a local store. There you will most likely find a selection of foods from around the world. It's incredible really—and it is a testament to how much the human race has evolved.

However, this is also a massive problem. The instant availability of convenience food comes at a price. More often than not, that food has travelled to the various warehouses and distribution centers by air. If you want food from exotic places, you must accept the travel required. Unfortunately, the amount of fossil fuel it takes to transport food across continents is incredible. These fossil fuels create greenhouse gases that directly contribute to the global warming that is damaging our planet.

You know when you buy apples and they look nice and shiny? Producers often use chemicals and waxes to create that shine and make their fruits and vegetables more attractive. Sadly, due to modern intensive farming techniques, the use of chemicals is not restricted to the presentation of foods. Growers use them in pesticides, fertilizers and growth hormones as well. When you consume them, your body retains them.

Buying genuine organic food is one way to guarantee you are not consuming these dangerous chemicals. The other is to grow your own. Doing so ensures that you know exactly what has gone into it—you know which fertilizers and other materials you have used to create that food. This not only stops your family from ingesting harmful chemicals but also helps the planet.

Once you start to grow your own produce, you will soon experience the excitement and anticipation of watching your garden progress. A rewarding and enjoyable pursuit, gardening is also educational, especially for any children in the household. Another aspect that you may not have considered is the health benefit of the physical activity required—and this is true even if you have limited mobility. There is a garden layout to suit every person and every outdoor space.

Different Gardening Methods

If you want to grow your own crops, you need to decide which method of gardening is the most suitable for your outdoor space and climate.

Containers

Container gardening is the most cost effective way to grow your own produce. It is suitable for areas as small as porches, balconies and even window boxes. Plenty of foods grow well in containers including:

- o Tomatoes
- o Strawberries
- o Green beans
- o Onions
- o Herbs

You'll also find many compact varieties of normally larger vegetable and fruit plants bred specifically for container gardening.

Container gardening equipment is not costly or complicated. Items you will need include:

- Soil
- Seeds
- Seedlings
- Planting containers
- Cages for tomatoes and any other plants that need support
- Gloves
- Gardening tools
- A watering can or hose

Sunlight will give you the optimum growing conditions, but you can also look into grow lamps. Recent developments in LED technology mean that you can run many of these lamps using considerably less energy than just one conventional sodium halide equivalent.

Growbags and boxes

If you don't want to bother with soil, growbags and boxes are a nice alternative to containers. However, they are not the most cost effective gardening option. You can only use a pre-packaged growbag once or twice before the plants deplete the growing material of its nutrients. Because you can compost a used growbag, it is still a sustainable option.

Raised beds and the foot technique

The typical raised bed is four feet by four feet square, at least six inches deep, and filled with soil. Cover the soil with weed control fabric, then take it foot by foot and divide the soil area into sixteen equal sections. Plant a different fruit or vegetable in each square. If you don't have the space for a traditional row garden, this is an excellent way to grow a wide variety of fruit and vegetables.

Traditional row gardening

This method demands the most space and plenty of sun for best results. (You can't move your garden to the optimum position as with the previous methods!) You must till the soil to get your garden off to the best start. This will remove weeds, stones, and break down soil clumps to aid root growth. Mix in a good variety of organic matter such as compost and manure. The organic materials you should use depend on the fruits or vegetables you are growing, so be sure to decide what you will be planting beforehand. Once tilled, you can plant a wonderful variety of traditional vegetables in rows six to ten inches apart.

What Should I Plant?

Once you have selected the gardening method that is right for you, the next step is to choose what you are going to plant. This is dependent on a number of factors, sadly not just what you like to eat most! First, you need to consider the climate of the area in which you live. Gardeners have divided the United States into several growing zones, which should give you a good idea of what you can grow.

When you buy seed packets, look for the growing zone and other instructions on the packaging. Follow these instructions if you want your garden to grow well.

However, the very best solution is to ask local growers about their experiences. They should be able to tell you what grows best in your geographical area.

The soil itself is important. If you do not know what type of soil you have, take a sample to your local plant nursery for analysis. Once analyzed, you will be able to tell what plants will grow. Some soil is ready for growing; other soil needs extra organic input.

Light—as in sunlight—is vital. You need to make sure that your new garden has plenty of it. This is quite a factor because many plants need copious quantities of natural sunshine. If you don't have this level of sunlight, find plants that can survive on a little less.

Get your stuff together

Get things organized. There are literally thousands of books on growing produce, not to mention numerous websites where you will find information on preparing and managing your garden. A great number of resources are available in this regard.

Online, for example, there are plenty of message boards and forums devoted to gardening. Join one to ask questions of those who are more experienced, or share your own insights.

If you take the time to source a local nursery that offers classes on gardening, you may find that this is the very best way to get real experience working the soil and growing your own produce. It is also a great way to make some friends.

Make sure you try to find other people who garden. They will have plenty of experience and be able to pass on their ideas to you.

What do you like?

Don't be swayed by what is fashionable in the media or other sources. You have to grow what you like. If you hate tomatoes but decide to grow them just because it is currently fashionable, you have wasted a lot of time and effort.

Having a garden allows you to try new things, and you never know what you may like. Try experimenting with different plants and crops. You may find that you discover new stuff that you like planting. When doing this, however, make sure that you only plant experimental crops in small amounts. You don't want to end up with crops you hate!

Natural Pest Control

You don't have to invest in hundreds of different pest control products that contain harmful chemicals. Using them will not only kill pests—there is a very good chance they will have a negative impact on your crop, too.

Try talking to the people down at your local nursery. They may be able to suggest some plants that naturally deter predators and pests. For example, marigolds actually deter many of the bugs that would normally lay waste to your crops.

Use chicken wire to keep out animals. A good set up of chicken wire will keep out rabbits and rodents—two types of pests that will do their best to rip up your crops and eat them. This is inexpensive stuff and should be easy to find in many hardware stores.

Squirrels have been a problem for decades in areas where people grow their own crops. There are now small electric fences you can use to keep them out of your garden. They only apply a slight shock as a deterrent, but they are very effective.

When it comes to grub worms or other such insects, you need to think about really organic stuff that works, such as bacteria. There is a variety called BT (*bacillus thuringiensis*) that really works to rid the garden of these little critters. It's a great solution to the pest problem because it kills insects effectively without harming humans. Take a visit to your nearest gardening or hardware store to find an easy to use solution.

Use natural predators, too. Dogs or cats can help to get rid of rodents like mice and rats. Ladybugs can help to rid your plants of aphids that would otherwise decimate the crop.

Remember that certain predators even be good news for your garden. Some insects actually help to pollinate the plants and decompose the soil—the humble earthworm is a perfect example.

Keep an eye on your garden, but leave pests alone unless they are actively ruining your crop. The natural life cycle on this planet has many elements.

Fertilization

While it is true that there are literally hundreds of commercially available fertilizers out there, it is not true that you have to buy them in order to have a great garden. There are some organic solutions that you can easily use to add nutrients to your soil.

If you live near a farm, you are in luck. Manure does an incredible job of helping plants to grow. Your local nursery may also have manure available.

Compost is another effective material you can use to fertilize soil. You can buy this from a store or create your own compost pile to produce it. Making your own allows you to do even more for the planet because it involves recycling your food waste, too.

So how do you actually make a compost pile? Well, surprisingly, it is not as hard or as complicated as you may think. First of all, you need an appropriate container. You can construct one from plywood or packing boxes. Once you've gathered your materials, make a container that is four feet by four feet.

Be aware that you will have to get your hands into the container to turn over your compost, so holes need to be big enough to make the material inside accessible. You also need a series of holes around the container so that the compost inside can be aerated.

Now comes the fun part: gathering your materials for composting. You'll find most of these in your regular household waste. Just look through your garbage bags and collect plenty of the following:

- Eggshells
- Rotten fruit and vegetables
- Dead plant material
- Dried leaves
- Coffee grounds

Animal products like old meat are a definite problem. These spoil, and once they are spoiled, they can house bacteria, which can compromise the health and safety of your home. Not only that, but meat scraps will attract unwanted four legged visitors, such as rats, foxes and bears.

Once you've placed the refuse in your compost pile, you need to add water to make it nice and moist. Don't go crazy here. Just add enough water for things to grow and thrive.

Remember to turn your compost regularly. This is an important part of the whole process, so get in there and get your hands dirty.

Compost piles are naturally warm because of the biological processing going on inside. If you don't think the bacteria are breaking down enough, buy some manufactured compost from your nearest garden store.

4

WHAT IF GARDENING ISN'T FOR ME?

Okay, we're not all avid gardeners. This is not a problem, and if you really don't like getting your hands dirty out in the garden, there are other options that you can consider to make sure you are doing your best with natural foods.

Buy local produce. Get down to your local farmer's market or farmer's store and buy foods grown in local fields and farms. This means they haven't travelled too far by air, which cuts down on the use of fossil fuels and helps the planet.

Farmer's markets are a relatively new phenomenon, and they have sprung up pretty much everywhere. Many farmers travel to urban areas to sell their wares in person as well.

If all that is still too difficult, your local supermarket may be able to help. They will often carry local produce in a section of the store that is clearly marked.

Get organic

Organic produce is good for you and the planet. It is worthwhile to source a good and local supplier of organic food. Unfortunately, organic produce found in typical grocery stores is not always what it seems. Instead, shop at a local organic food store. This way you will know that the stuff hasn't travelled too far—and that it is what it says it is.

Unfortunately, organic food often has to travel a long way to get to the supermarket—using huge amounts of fossil fuel in the process. However, organic is still a better all-round choice if you can't grow your own or buy local produce.

Join a co-op

You could also join a co-op, where you pay a monthly or weekly fee to buy a share of the harvest from a farm cooperative.

This means you will get a box of fresh produce each month or week. This includes great in season fruits and vegetables, making co-ops a popular option for those who cannot grow their own.

Some co-ops actually allow you to participate in the growing and harvesting as well. The experience can be quite rewarding because you get to feel what it is like to grow your own produce.

The intimacy thing

When you think about it, we have an incredibly intimate relationship with the food that we put into our body. It is for the best that we work hard to get it right, both for the planet and ourselves. We share our insides with food; why not make sure that it is the cleanest, healthiest food available?

5

KEEPING YOUR OWN LIVESTOCK

This chapter may not have the same appeal for everyone who reads this book. Basically, we can divide the world into those who like animal products and those who don't. If you are not a meat eater, skip this chapter.

One of the key reasons people chose to rear their own food animals is to ensure ethical treatment. Mass-market farms around the world put hundreds of thousands of animals through inhumane experiences every year. When you raise your own livestock, you reduce this number.

Diet is important. Making sure that your animals have the correct diet for their nutritional needs is vital. They also need to be able to move around freely. On many unethical mass-market farms, they do not get this opportunity.

Other factors are included under the diet heading. If you feed your animals too much corn, you can increase their risk of contracting E coli. It is vitally important that anyone who rears animals look after this aspect of their care.

When you rear chickens on a natural diet, and give them plenty of room to move around, they are much less likely to carry excess fat.

This turns them into healthier birds and healthier food for your family too.

Antibiotics

Mass-market farms often raise animals, like chickens, close together. As a result, they must give them antibiotics because they contract infections. However, this means that the people who end up consuming these birds are eating food that contains a high level of antibiotics.

Incredibly, this situation can lead to drug resistance. With a higher level of antibiotics in our body than normal, the bacteria that cause disease become more resistant to treatment. This means we require even stronger does of antibiotics to combat illness.

It doesn't get any better the deeper you dig. If we raise animals in unsafe atmospheres such as feedlots, the food that they eventually produce is also unsafe. Put it this way: the bacterial levels found in food produced commercially are much higher than in food produced by individuals.

The environment

We all know that waste products from cows—methane gas, for example—pollute the atmosphere. This causes many problems and affects the safety of our planet.

The unsafe disposal of waste products from farm animals is also widespread. Add to this the fact that the care of the animals is poor and you have even more evidence that mass-market farming directly affects the environment.

Poor conditions for people, too

The working conditions on some of the larger farms are often pitiful, putting human lives in danger with faulty machinery, cramped spaces and a host of other problems. It is also a well-known fact that some large farms and factories take advantage of migrant workers.

Doing it yourself

As mentioned earlier, many people are now choosing to rear their own animals—and doing so is actually easier than you may think. While you many believe that you don't have enough space or resources to raise your own, the reality is often far from this.

Chickens

Believe it or not, it is now easier than ever to set up your own chicken coop, even in urban areas. Many cities and towns are now allowing people to raise chickens without any fuss. However, it is always best to check first, just to be sure that the local laws allow you to do this.

The best thing about raising chickens is the egg that you can have daily, right out of your backyard. Obviously, you may also choose to harvest the meat, using some of your chickens in this way.

Your first job is to sort out the accommodation for the chickens. You can use chicken wire and wood to build your own coop. Your biggest concern should be making sure that the chickens have a reasonable amount of space in which to move around.

Then you need to get your hands on some chicks. There are plenty of local suppliers that can provide you with young, healthy specimens. You can also use the Internet to search for chick suppliers, and you should find a good source pretty quickly.

Get to know other people who raise chickens because they are often the very best source of information. You will find that they are only too happy to share tips and ideas that will help you.

Goats

If you have ever seen goats at a local petting zoo, you know just how playful and lively they are. Great fun to have around, they also prove to be excellent livestock.

You will have to check the local laws to make sure goat rearing is allowed in your neighborhood. Once you have done this, make sure that you have the proper shelter for your goats. These animals are famous for being a little pesky so you will certainly need an escape proof pen.

Your local agriculture extension is an excellent source of help and support in raising goats, as are other people you know who have already given it a try.

Cows and Pigs

Now this is getting serious—cows and pigs are certainly a step up from chickens and goats. You need to make sure the laws in your area allow you to raise large animals like this. And on top of all that, you need to arrange for adequate space. Don't expect to raise cows in the city.

The best thing about raising livestock of this size is the production of meat that is free of hormones and antibiotics. It's much healthier than any you'll find at mass-market farms and factories. You can also make sure that the animals have nice lives free from stress and duress.

Cows give milk, which also allows you to make cheese and butter. And of course, you can also harvest this livestock for beef.

Pigs are also excellent. A good pork sausage can become a staple of your diet if you raise pigs well. You can even make your own hams and other healthy pork products. Some people find rearing pigs easier than cows, too.

You can slaughter and then butcher your own animals if you like, but there is another option. Take them to a meat processor and support a business in your local community.

Other Options

You don't have to limit your livestock to cows, pigs, goats and chickens. There are many other options you can investigate to widen the scope of your farm and bring in some great produce as well.

Rabbits are great for meat and fur; they are also easy to look after. Sheep, which produce meat and wool, are easy to care for as well. You can rear geese, turkey and pheasant for meat, too.

Obviously, check your local laws before purchasing any livestock. Most areas have different regulations, and they're worth knowing before you jump in.

Look at things differently

One major challenge that people—and especially families—face is the mindset that comes with animals, especially young ones.

If you grew up in a city or town, and your main experience with animals was pets, then you may find it difficult to come around to the idea that you are going to be raising them for slaughter.

Do not form an emotional attachment to the animals. Raising them in your backyard will be impossible if you think of them as part of your family.

If you grew up on a farm, you may be used to a way of life that promotes the use of livestock for slaughter. If you are going to raise your own livestock, try the following tips to prevent unnecessary attachment:

- o Don't name them. If you do, they become part of your family.
- o Don't let them into your home.
- o If you have children, explain carefully what having livestock means.

At the same time, make sure you respect the animals. You don't have to treat them roughly just because you are trying to remain detached. Your responsibility is to care for their needs fully.

If Keeping Livestock Is Not Practical

If you live in an urban area, you may not be able to raise livestock. However, there could be another reason why you are not going to exercise the option. For some people, it is just not something they want to do.

If you're just not ready to raise animals in this way, there are other things you can do to help save the planet. These other options also go a long way towards creating a much healthier lifestyle than the one you have previously enjoyed.

Going local

Get online and have a good look at local areas. You may find farms that actually sell their livestock to community members like you. This is because farmers are realizing that local produce makes more sense, financially and ethically.

There is a nice feeling attached to buying local meat products. An online search can help you find suppliers who can also arrange for collection or delivery.

You will even have the opportunity to visit the farm and see where they are raising the animals. This allows you some peace of mind, as you can determine if they are receiving humane treatment. You can also get a chance to speak with the farmer.

Visit a local farmer's market and take the opportunity to schedule the delivery of food from local providers. Many farmers now make a sizeable percentage of their livelihood from markets; buying from them helps a community business, too.

Buy a whole animal, or at least a larger part than you would in a local supermarket. You can then freeze the parts that you aren't quite ready to use. This means that you can spread out the cost of meals over a significant amount of time, and it allows you to eat for less overall.

Organic

As with fruit and vegetables, you can also go organic. Most supermarkets now stock organic meats as part of their inventory. These are free from hormones and other harmful chemicals, and they are a good alternative if you can't find a farmer's market.

You can also pick up milk produced by cows on an organic diet so you gain an even better deal health wise.

Think about cutting down your meat intake. While this is not an obvious way to reduce damage to the environment, cutting down on the meat that we eat means we are using less overall.

If you cut down meat consumption by at least one or two days a week, you will be surprised at how much of a difference it can make to your carbon footprint.

Sustainable living has a massive impact upon our environment. However, it is not something that you have to spend years organizing. In fact, simple small steps can make a big difference. Take the example of buying organic.

If you want to raise your own animals, don't go all the way too quickly and start with cows. Pick chickens first, taking the time to learn the best way to raise them. This will give you a taste for the discipline of raising livestock and will be great fun, too.

And remember that raising your own animals is not necessary. You can investigate farmers markets and look at buying organic food that helps nearly as much as raising your own livestock. These are all positive options.

Doing this kind of thing might seem like a small step, but if you do it enough, your local community will start to see the benefit of your sustainable living.

Of course, you could give up meat and dairy completely—becoming a vegan. However, this is not always the best option for everyone, and don't feel you have to do this. Eating ethically produced meat goes a long way towards helping the planet and preserving your health.

6

ENERGY SOURCES AND CONSUMPTION

One absolutely essential part of sustainable living on our planet is making sure that we do our very best to use energy in a sensible way in our homes. This means looking at ways to conserve energy usage. One thing that can help us get better at this is to understand where the energy actually comes from. This chapter will look carefully at all aspects of this key area.

Some energy sources are actually more sustainable than others. While it is pretty much impossible to stop using energy altogether, we can still take a good look at our energy resources and attempt to find ways to cut down usage in increments.

Fossil Fuels

When we drive our cars, we are using fossil fuel sources to power their engines. We also use fossil fuels in the generation of electricity and other power sources.

Fossil fuels are the particular type of fuel that we find as part of the natural resources of our planet. They can come in a liquid, solid or gas form. The liquid and gas elements come from dead animals that have decomposed. This process takes a lot of time.

Fossil fuels also include oil and natural gas, and we use large drills to find them. These machines can be bad for the environment as well as dangerous for the people who have to use them. In fact, there have been a number of huge disasters caused by the use of machinery necessary to discover oil and natural gas.

Plants that are dead help to produce coal. The remains of these plants have petrified and rotted over millions of years. We get coal from deep underground. Many of us are aware of the dangers involved in mining, and it is one of the most hazardous jobs in the world.

All of this fossil fuel use really plays a big part in air pollution. When we burn fuel, it gives off carbon dioxide. What is more, all this waste is really for nothing because fossil fuels are nonrenewable. Once gone, they are irreplaceable. Unfortunately, we use them a lot.

Solar

The sun is both a powerful ally and a danger. For centuries, people have worked to find ways to harness this power. The main aim has been to try and convert it into electricity.

Take a look at the nearest home that has solar panels—it is using passive solar energy. Passive solar includes structures built specifically to take in and use the energy from the sun.

Photovoltaic cells utilize active solar energy to power electronic devices and machines—most famously, the solar calculator. However, they are now becoming even more common in large structures and machines.

The best thing about solar energy is that it has no waste asset. It leaves no pollutants behind after its use. It is totally clean. It does have some drawbacks, however, that make it a questionable source of energy for some people.

Solar power is expensive. The problem is not a fossil fuel problem—we can't deplete the sun—but we are still spending a lot of money on it. The equipment we need to make it all happen costs a lot of money. And when you're talking about surface area for units, it's big.

Wind

Over the last few centuries, people have been using windmills to harness the wind and make energy from it. It has long been a reliable and popular source of energy and production.

Like the energy from the sun, wind energy is completely renewable; we don't deplete it when we use it. But again, like the sun, it costs a lot of money to create the machinery and run the systems to harness wind energy.

You need large flat areas to create wind farms. This has often meant rural or coastal locations.

The loudness and unsightly appearance of wind farms—with hundreds of turbines dotted around the nearby landscape—have led to a number of complaints as they have become more common.

However, some people have actually bought their own personal windmills to power their homes. They do cost a lot of money initially, but they are great energy savers in the long run.

The bigger electrical companies that provide commercial power to homes and businesses often use wind power to harness electricity.

Water

Windmills use wind energy to turn turbines, and water farms use water to do the same job. If you are unconvinced that this is a powerful tool, just note the Hoover Dam. It has made use of such technology for a very long time.

Water farms are changing the ecosystem because rivers and other water sources need to be dammed in the process. However, it is a very cost-effective source of power.

Dams often have hatcheries nearby. This allows for the farming of native fish and their reintroduction to the ecosystem, which is definitely beneficial. However, some damage to the natural ecosystem is unavoidable when we harness waterpower.

Nuclear

This is a very controversial source of power. In fact, there are often events—from leaks to massive disasters—that have given this particular power source a very bad name in the media.

Recent events at a huge nuclear plant in Japan have caused people to question the validity of nuclear power, primarily because there are huge safety concerns if things do go wrong. Radiation exposure is a definite danger for local citizens and workers.

The waste that a nuclear power plant produces is also a significant concern. It can affect the environment for years after it enters the atmosphere.

On top of that, the safe storage of nuclear waste is a major problem. There are always issues around how a government might store the waste from nuclear power usage.

Bio-Fuels

Many of the organisms on our planet contain bio-fuel. Burning wood can release bio-fuel, and there has been a recent movement towards burning trash to create certain bio-fuels.

Bio-fuel research scientists have recently studied both corn and soy and are also looking at algae as a potential source of bio-fuel.

Bio-fuel converters retrofitted in cars allow these vehicles to run on substances like vegetable oils. The engines run incredibly clean and are very easy to maintain. However, you will not find one at your average car dealership yet.

While scientists have long considered bio-fuels a potential solution to the environmental crisis, some worry that their use could lead to a food shortage.

Reducing Energy Dependence

When it comes to reducing the energy drain in your home there are a multitude of smart choices you can make on a daily basis. This involves thinking carefully about how and where you use energy. It also involves working hard to cut down massively across all areas so that overall usage is low.

Seeing the light

You may well have become a little uneasy as you witness the massive drain on energy represented by the sheer number of light bulbs surrounding us. There are so many that are used every day, even in just our homes, that it can seem an impossible task to make a dent in this massive outlay of energy. Many lights used in commercial settings, for example, are on 24 hours a day. This represents incredible wastage.

At home, make it a mission to turn off any lights that you don't need at the time. This can mean literally walking around your residence to see if anyone has left unnecessary lights on. There are special motion sensor units you can install to shut them off automatically. These are not expensive, and they do a great job of helping you to ensure that your energy use is appropriate. They also prevent you from having to think too much about turning lights off as you move around your home.

Incandescent bulbs are a thing of the past. The common way of thinking these days is to use bulbs that actively help to save the environment. Much of the energy used by an old-fashioned incandescent bulb is lost through heat, which is an incredible waste of good energy.

Fluorescent and LED lighting have become the new norm for good energy usage and efficiency. While they may not have produced the best-looking bulbs in recent years, manufacturers are now developing versions for home use that are more attractive and in keeping with the average family's décor. They also last a lot longer and use up less energy than standard lighting.

In the daytime, make it a point to use natural light more often. This will ensure that you are not overusing artificial lighting that takes up energy.

World of electronics

Our world is full of electronics, from televisions to computers to iPods. There's no way to turn back time and become less dependent on this equipment for work and home. However, you can make some smart decisions to minimize your carbon footprint.

Set computers and tablets to energy saver mode. This will allow your monitor to turn off when you're not really using the computer. You should also turn off, or hibernate, machines when they're not going to be in use for long periods.

When you leave the office for the weekend, turn off the computer. Many people leave computers running all the time, and this drains energy unnecessarily. This can be true in homes as well.
When you buy large appliances, look for items that have energy star ratings. These use less to do their job. Not only will this save energy, it can also save you quite a bit of money on your utility bills. In addition, there are some tax breaks for purchasing appliances with this rating.

Heating and Cooling

Amazingly, much of your monthly household energy bill comes from just two things: heating and cooling. Fortunately, sustainable living isn't about going to extremes; you don't have to give up your air conditioning or heat. Instead, making small changes can dramatically reduce the overall cost and benefit the environment.

When it is hot in the summer, let your thermostat work a little harder than you would normally expect it to. Most people try to maintain an average temperature, but make it work a little harder and you should find measurable results in the general coolness of the place.

There are also plenty of other things that you can do to keep your home cooler in the summer without wasting a lot of money on energy.

- Close curtains and blinds during the day when the heat from the sun has the biggest impact.
- Use the fans in the room rather than the thermostat. Use ceiling fans and oscillating fans, but don't forget to turn them off when you leave the room.
- Think about what you are wearing.
- Don't use the oven too much because this builds up heat. Instead, cook outside or eat a cold meal.
- When it comes to bedding, use lighter linens that won't make you feel hot

In the winter, saving energy is even easier. This means a little common sense and some hard work will keep you from wasting money.

- Invest in thermal curtains for your windows. These trap heat and help to make the home warmer.
- Add to the sheets and linen you have on your beds. You can use down comforters and flannel sheets.
- Wear slippers for extra warmth at home.
- Going back to the windows, use insulation film to make the home warmer.
- Block drafts with weather stripping around windows and doors.
- Exterior doors are a key spot for drafts. Place a rolled up towel at the base of the door to keep the heat in.

Windows are responsible for a lot of energy wastage in homes. If you have not already done so, counteract this by installing double pane windows to keep in the heat. While they may be relatively expensive to install, they will pay for themselves in the savings on energy usage. When having new windows fitted, do your research and request quotes from several companies.

Utilities and Planning

Utilities

Look into the utility companies in your area because some have actively sought to use renewable sources of energy. This may mean more cost in the short term, but you will save long term—and save the planet, too.

Blank canvas

If you have the opportunity to build your own new home, think about the possibility of sustainable planning. You need to consider the direction your home will face as well as other issues, such as landscaping. Of course, the placement of windows, and their fitting, can have a huge impact on your energy usage and sustainability.

Get the windows insulated so you save energy in the long run. You can also ask for specially insulated walls, which will help drive down the cost of heating. Since you are in control of the build, you can look at more energy efficient cooling and heating systems, too.

Ask the experts

When you are really into making a big effort to live more sustainably, it is always a good idea to get professionals involved. Learning what they think about your plan is both a powerful motivator and a great chance to gain insight.

A consultant will come into your home and have a good look around to find ways in which they think you can cut down on energy wastage. This will really help you as you work towards making your home even more sustainable.

Transportation Energy

Transportation is a massive drain on energy resources on this planet. It is easy to say that you want to cut down on the costs and carbon impact of transportation, but getting this bit right is not always simple.

Rather than stay indoors all day, which some people think is a viable way to reduce their carbon footprint, some small changes in the right areas will help just as much.

Increase those walks

Walking is one of the key areas in which we can reduce our carbon footprint—though it's also one we tend to neglect. We can and should walk much of the day. Even if you believe you are too far from school or work to walk, you should still investigate the possibility.

When it comes to supermarket shopping, consider walking rather than driving. This is not always feasible due to the number of bags you need to carry, but a walk to the local grocery store makes much more sense, for example, than driving.

Some communities have developed the concept of a "walking school bus." This is where a number of adult volunteers walk children to school. Obviously, if you have a neighborhood that is pro-pedestrian, with crossings and so on, this is an option worth investigating.

Pedal power

Think about cycling to work or school. This is one of the more powerful ways to reduce your carbon footprint, simply due to the fact that it is great for your health and a lot of fun to do. Make sure your bike is road safe first.

Share that car

Carpools have long been the best way to solve the problem of carbon waste from vehicles. You take turns driving other people to school or work, sharing a car. It becomes a great social event and does wonders for the environment.

Organization is required, as you will need to set up a schedule and get other drivers involved. Many people choose a specific day of the week as their turn to drive. You could divide the month week by week.

If there is only one person with a car that is large enough for many passengers, just split the fuel costs.

Public transportation

Not enough people take advantage of public transportation, yet many towns and cities have great networks to help you get where you need to be efficiently.

Trains and subways are even better than buses because there are no traffic issues. The overall cost year on year is less than using a car. If you speak to the local transportation companies, you can often find great monthly discounts.

Ask your employers about company discounts for using public transportation as well. As more embrace sustainable business practices, you may find more savings than you expected.

Efficient vehicles

This is one of the most obvious ways in which you can really reduce the family carbon footprint. Look around for a budget-friendly vehicle that is more energy efficient than most. Cars are becoming greener every year.

There are also many vehicles that run on flex fuels or natural gas. These burn cleaner and gain much more in the way of mileage. They are more expensive, due to the build cost involved, so take a good look at your finances before making the investment.

We all love our Internet and other modern conveniences, but you don't necessarily have to give up these luxuries if you want to live in a more carbon-friendly world.

You only need to make small changes so that you don't end up wasting a lot of energy. And small steps overall make the whole thing less painful. Get the whole family on board if you want to make things even easier.

Frank Randall

7

SUSTAINING THE EARTH BY MANAGING WASTE

Reduce, reuse, recycle

Our planet faces many problems when it comes to waste, but one of the biggest is consumption and the consequent disposal of items. As a race, we are more likely to throw something away than fix it.

One of the key principles in sustainability is to use what we have to the furthest extent, recycle what we no longer need, and try our very best to repurpose what we have used so that we can reuse it.

Reduce

Ask yourself if you have more in your life than you actually need. Take a look in the closet and work out which items you haven't worn for a long while. Most people have stuff they never wear. If you want to brave it, ask yourself if you have entire rooms in your home that are essentially closets—not to mention the garage.

You need to look carefully at the storage you are using, and ask yourself if your general consumption of goods is way too much. You don't have to cut down massively, just take a look at what you have and ask yourself if it is reasonable.

Factories often produce items with non-renewable sources of energy. This means the more stuff we buy the more we harm the planet. This also means that you need more space to store the items.

The more space you have the more energy you need to heat and cool it. And the more stuff you buy the more you just throw away, adding to landfills.

Consider these tips for consuming less:

- Before you buy clothes, ask yourself if you could use the same items again in other outfits. The more versatile your wardrobe, the more effective it is.
- Do your best to buy clothing made from sustainable fabrics, meaning those created from greener materials.
- When shopping in stores, make a list before you leave home, and then stick to that list.
- Try to buy items that serve more than one purpose.
- Before you go out and spend money on anything new, take a look around your home. Is there anything there that can be used for the same purpose you are about to spend on?

The curse of disposable products

We all love disposable products—the usually make our life a lot easier. Having them around isn't always something we can avoid. Unfortunately, the sheer number of these little helpers has ballooned over the past few decades. Consider:

- Diapers
- Eating utensils

- Cups
- Plates
- Napkins
- Cameras
- Razors
- Towels
- Sanitary products
- Makeup applicators
- Cat litter boxes
- Coffee filters
- Bottled water
- Air filters
- Sandwich bags (and other packaging)
- Paper bags
- Baby wipes
- And the list could go on and on

However, if we look at that list very carefully, we can see that there is usually an alternative to every item on it. If it is not an alternative product, it is an alternative use. No matter how much we love disposable products, we may well have to start thinking about saying goodbye to them if we are to have a positive impact upon our environment. Trading them in for items that are made from renewable resources is one of the most popular and practical ways to help the planet.

Reuse

Before you pick up an item and throw it in the trashcan, think carefully. Make sure that the trashcan is the very best place for it, for example. Many items can now be reused or repurposed; you don't have to throw them away.

Next time you are at the grocery store and bring home a lot of plastic bags, you need to think twice before throwing them away. For example, instead of tossing those plastic bags use them as trashcan liners, containers for cleaning out the litter box, or for carrying groceries another time.

Better yet, use bags that aren't designed to be thrown away. It's becoming more and more popular to buy reusable shopping bags for groceries and other items. You can use these things over and over again.

Take a look at the furniture in your home, too. The older things that are lying around are only dated, and this means you can update them with a good polish or a little paint. You can easily create a house full of what is basically reconditioned furniture.

When it comes to your clothing, think about updating an outfit rather than buying a new one. You would be surprised to learn just how many people throw away clothes that they could easily turn into something new.

Your aim should be to work hard to reuse items again and again. This seems quite challenging, but it is most certainly possible with some self-discipline. Use real dishes instead of paper plates when you are hosting a party or cookout. Buy permanent filters for coffee machines. Not all of this may seem like the biggest deal in the world, but your planet is suffering due to the fact that many people do not seem to understand the wastefulness of disposable living. Here are some options for reusing items rather than wastefully disposing of them:

- o Use permanent handled razors instead of disposables.
- o Use cloth diapers that can be washed and reused.
- o Use feminine products that can be washed and reused.
- o Recover furniture when the pattern goes out of style.

- Repaint cabinets and update hardware instead of buying new.
- Move furniture from one part of the house to another room to give it a fresh look.
- Use glass storage containers instead of disposable packaging.
- Use a pitcher with a filter instead of bottled water.
- Use washcloths instead of baby wipes.

While it is obviously the best-case scenario to reuse everything that you can, some people are not able to do this so easily. The way around this is to stop relying on disposable stuff so often. Reduce your dependence on these items and you will see a corresponding reduction in waste.

Take a careful look at the disposable items in your home, and then work out which of them you simply cannot do without. You're not likely to find very many, and this very simple step will have a significant impact on your overall waste.

For example, you can reuse heavily stained clothing as cleaning cloths for your home. You can remake furniture or at least reupholster it. A good clean goes a very long way.

Recycle

This has become both more popular and easier to do in recent years. This is because governments worldwide have helpfully put systems in place to make recycling easier and faster. The most obvious and widely recycled items are those made of paper and plastic. People are now more readily recycling glass items, too. What's more, urban recycling is even easier now that many towns offer curbside collection. You walk less and recycle more.

Of course, you may have to make the trip to a recycling center. This is not such a big chore when you consider what you are doing to help the environment. There are now many recognized places where you can do this.

You will find that there are many items that can now be recycled including:

- Pizza boxes
- Water bottles
- Glass beer and wine bottles
- Paper
- Cardboard boxes
- Milk jugs and cartons
- Aluminum cans
- Grocery sacks (paper and plastic)
- Aluminum foil
- Soda bottles
- Shampoo bottles
- Lotion bottles

Plastic items even make it easier for you. The have numbers on their bases. These numbers help you to understand which can be recycled and which cannot:

- 1 and 2 are almost always accepted by recycling programs
- 3, 6 and 7 are generally not accepted
- 4 and 5 are sometimes accepted, but you'll need to ask the program

Taking part in a recycling program is important. They will offer much more information on which items can be recycled and which cannot. They will also let you know which items they can only accept under certain conditions.

Water bottles are recyclable, but the lids aren't always. Some programs will take them with lids while others won't. Check the guidelines and make sure that you are following the rules.

Don't forget composting. We discussed this in some detail earlier in the book. This practice helps you to deal with waste that comes from the kitchen naturally. It also stops foodstuff from going into landfills.

Making recycling part of your daily routine makes it a whole lot easier to do. People like stuff to be easy, and if you have a daily routine that recycling fits into, it will be. Make sure, for example, that you have a lot of containers ready in your kitchen. These can be used for:

- Trash
- Recycling
- Compost

If you are near a center that requires you to sort items first, you will also need containers for:

- Glass
- Plastic
- Paper/cardboard
- Aluminum

Sort all of this stuff out immediately after using it. Putting items directly into the proper container will cut down on mess as well. And because they are all ready, it won't take long to transport them.

Electronics recycling

When it comes to electronics, things are a little more complicated. You will have to consider a couple of things before you dive into recycling. For example, many electronic items have heavy metals in them that will need removal. There is also the possibility that there will be parts involved.

Target, Best Buy and other retailers often offer drop-off centers for electronic recycling. If you have an old cellphone, for example, you may find a special bin where you can drop it off. Online, you will find special sites that take phones and give them to charities.

Computers are always an issue because it is not that easy to recycle them. Some centers won't take them so you need to work around this. Contact thrift stores and see if they will accept them. If they don't, they can often point you in the direction of a local place that will. However, you may need to pay a fee.

When All Else Fails…Donate

Donating to charities feels good, and it does a lot for the environment, too. If you have large quantities of stuff at home, and you can't otherwise get rid of it, consider donating. Excellent donation items include:

- Furniture
- Clothing
- Baby items
- Toys
- Books
- CDs
- Appliances
- Cookware
- Dishes
- Vases
- Decorative items
- Jewelry
- Automobiles
- Electronics

You will be giving these things a new home and also benefitting the charity. To get the best out of an experience like this, research your local area for charities that actually mean something to you. Local thrift stores benefit all kinds of charities and causes including domestic abuse shelters, food pantries and homeless shelters.

Craigslist is a good example of a place online that will help you get rid of unwanted stuff through donation. You can even make a bit of money when you sell unwanted goods through such a service. Whatever you do, the item isn't going to a landfill, which always helps the environment.

Don't think that some people wouldn't want your items. They most certainly might. Some people prize what others see as disposable, broken or otherwise meaningless stuff.

Keeping the world clutter free

One of the scariest images for anyone who is trying to be sustainable is the sight of a barge taking landfill to another country. United States citizens have a duty to cut down on waste, and you need to understand that one of the biggest threats to our very existence is the amount of it we produce.

If you take steps to reduce what you buy, reduce what you have, and recycle as much as you can of what you use, you can make a massive impact on our planet. This does mean a change in lifestyle, but the impact is incredible.

The process enables you to reduce clutter as well. Your home can be a nightmare if it has too much clutter in it. Reducing and reusing goes a long way to getting rid of that claustrophobic feeling.

Keeping Poisons Out of the Landfill

Getting rid of toxic waste

While we would all love the freedom to recycle everything we have in our homes, some items obviously deserve special attention. We can't rid ourselves of them, but we can at least teach ourselves to get rid of them properly. They can be toxic and dangerous for the planet, so extra care is needed.

Items that fall into this category include:

- Paints
- Solvents
- Used batteries
- Motor oil

Throw these away in the trash or flush them down drains and you are asking for trouble. The stuff can be dangerous to people and the wider environment. Thankfully, most cities provide special places where you can dispose of them properly.

Most recycling centers have special bays for paints and solvents as well as other toxic items such as batteries. If you're looking at auto parts, most auto stores offers services in this area.

If you don't have a local center for the disposal of items like these, you can often find one within a few miles. Some larger cities even accept items from smaller places for a fee—enabling everyone to share the load.

Get online and find the nearest place that will take your hazardous waste. They shouldn't be too far away. While it is not the easiest and most convenient thing in the world to get rid of this waste, it will help to save the planet.

Medications

Go to the family medicine cabinet and you will most likely find a vast array of medicines. These great little helpers assist with everyday living from pain relief to vitamins. However, disposing of them is not so simple. You have to practice care here, too.

Your local pharmacist can give you some sound ideas about how best to dispose of the medicines you have in your cabinet. They may even allow you to drop them off for disposal.

The DEA also run programs around the country for safe disposal of such items. This means that the whole thing works on two fronts by not only keeping your family safe, but also the environment.

If you have teenage children in the home, think twice about keeping any medication within easy reach. Some drugs, such as muscle relaxants, hold a particular attraction for this age range and can have very harmful side effects.

Making it easy on yourself

Like most of the sustainable habits listed in this book, keeping waste sensible is just a matter of taking small steps to build up systems that will allow you to take charge of these vital aspects of home life.

One thing you could do is choose a safe place in your home where you can store all the hazardous waste materials prior to getting rid of them. Keep them in containers, such as an especially strong one for batteries, and so on.

Make the disposal of hazardous materials a regular thing, and take them to the relevant centers at the same time once every two months or so. You could also make sure that part of your routine is to check the medicine cabinet every six months. This way you won't have medication lingering in there that could be disposed of safely.

One other simple thing you could try to make the problem easier to manage is to limit the number of hazardous materials that you have in your home in the first place—reducing your need for worry. Your disposal can be more organized and help the environment, too.

Frank Randall

8

GETTING KIDS INVOLVED WITH YOUR NEW LIFESTYLE

Fun for the whole family

You need to get the kids involved with the whole process, too. It can be great fun and very rewarding to care for the environment. The sooner kids realize this, the better. There are a lot of benefits to getting the children involved in the process of improving the world.

Why kids should get involved

There are many reasons why kids would benefit from helping you to help the environment. You need to instill an appreciation of these benefits at a young age.

Kids who participate in sustainable living are:

- More likely to learn important gardening skills and develop a taste for vegetables
- Prone to getting the recycling bug
- Going to be healthier physically, due to the fresh air and good food they take in
- More likely to want to promote better treatment for animals
- Less likely to have any kind of wish to develop a lifestyle

where physical possessions are important

The real rewards come when the children actually volunteer to help with the environmentally friendly chores. If they help with this, you get a chance to step back and let someone else do the work. This is immensely satisfying because you are not only getting a break, but also helping the children learn.

Making sustainable living fun

If your aim is to try your very best to make sure that your kids are also enjoying sustainable living, then there are a few things you can put in place to make this a reality. Get them to participate in the process with some of the following suggestions.

- Ask your kids to dust off their outdoor clothes and get out into the garden. They can plant crops and plants with you. There are a few varieties that kids really love planting.
- Take the time to build and create recycling centers for the children in your home. Put pictures on them so the kids get a real feel for what they are all about.
- Get your kids to help you paint or rebuild your old furniture so it can be reused or sold.
- If you have animals on your property, make their care part of a series of chores for your children.
- Believe it or not, some children actually want to sew. So teach them.
- Get those fresh vegetables out and encourage children to gain knowledge in their cooking and the reasons why we need to use resources like this.
- Sit in on some nights with the family and discuss the planet, its problems, and what we can do to help.
- As a family, get out in the garden and plant some trees. It's great fun, and the kids love it.
- Go to thrift stores with your children and encourage them to think about their purchases.
- Volunteer with your kids; talk to them about the choices they make when they volunteer.
- When sorting out your gardening or farming, get the children

out there to help you plan the space and how it is going to be used.
- Make it your business to source and read children's stories about the environment and looking after it.

The real reward here is something that may well be less tangible to you, at least at the outset. When you teach your children to become even more sustainable in their own everyday lives, then you are giving them a life skill that they will use for years to come, long after you have gone. This has massive implications for the planet now and in the future.

At first, your kids may not want to participate. However, they will eventually start to understand the value of what you are teaching them. You should see some results very soon that will make it all seem worthwhile.

Let them understand that what they are doing is going to help others—including the planet. Make them feel happy and excited by giving them lots of opportunities to enjoy what they are doing.

Frank Randall

9

22 OF THE BIGGEST LIFESTYLE TIPS

Some small steps may be better to get things started slowly and take the pressure off. There are several quick and easy steps that you can take immediately to transform the way you see the planet and your place on it.

You can make all of these changes or pick just one or two. Even just one small change can add a lot of value to the planet. You can really make a massive impact on your world if you do just a couple of small things.

Once you have one habit firmly in place, you should find it easier to get things really moving. You can keep going on and on until you are doing a massive amount of work to help the planet.

- Plant a tree; choose one and just plant it.
- Buy a pitcher system for water.
- Get out to the back garden and hit the porch. You can create an herb garden there.
- Buy vegetables from local farmers.
- Head out to your local supermarket and buy only organic vegetables.
- Vinegar is a completely natural cleaner. Use this to clean your house.

- Get the discipline of redoing old furniture firmly locked into your mindset. Often it is only a paint job that is needed.
- Open up your closet and throw away any clothes that you don't use.
- Fluorescent and LED light bulbs are the future. Use them.
- Don't throw any paper away. Recycle or reuse it.
- Investigate the use of motion sensors for lighting. They can save you thousands over just a few years.
- Recycle cans. This kind of behavior helps to save your planet.
- Use plastic grocery sacks as trash can liners. They are really effective in this regard.
- Remodeling your home is exciting, but it is even more fun when you use renewable sources like bamboo for flooring.
- Whenever you can, buy items made from recyclable materials.
- Once you have finished your medication program, take the old bottles back to the pharmacy.
- In the winter, use thermal curtains at the windows.
- One of our biggest resources is natural light. Use it during the day rather than the light bulb.
- When next headed out to the store, walk.
- Give your car, and the planet, a break when travelling to work. Take the bus.
- Create a carpool. It saves the planet.
- Animals for meat need transporting, and this means fuel waste. Choose one day in your week to go vegetarian.

Any one of these choices can help to protect the planet. Doing something—even if it's small—is better than doing nothing to conserve Earth's resources. With every positive change you make you are working toward making the planet healthier and preserving it for future generations.

If you're not ready to overhaul your entire lifestyle, taking it one step at a time can be beneficial. In the next chapter, we'll look at how to make a plan for a more sustainable future for you and your family.

10

SET A GOAL AND MAKE YOUR PLAN

A plan really makes a huge difference when you are trying to make sustainable living part of your reality. Whenever you start to make changes like this to your lifestyle, you need to have some kind of plan in place. This is because it helps to make your journey to sustainability a lot more pleasant.

Set a goal

You need to have a goal before you start on the path towards sustainable living. For example, some people decide that they want to make their life more sustainable because they want to save money. This is perhaps the most common goal for many people. They don't hate the environment; they care about it. But they also know that they can gain extra income through savings made by making their lives more sustainable.

You may want to grow your own food. It may be an absolute dream of yours to make your own food plot a reality in your life. You may even want to take it a step further and work towards raising livestock on your land. This is a big step, but it may be something you've dreamt about since childhood.

Your job is to make sure that you know exactly what you want from your future. This means taking a good look at what you want from your world as well. If you want a happier and cleaner world, then work towards that. If you want to save money, then work towards that as a valuable goal. Whatever you choose to do, make sure that the goal is something that is appropriate to your life.

Making your plan

Once your goal is in place you need to set up a plan. You start by taking a good look at where you would like the whole thing to end. Within five years, would you like to be living a completely self-sustaining lifestyle? Work out what you need to do each year to make sure that you reach that goal.

Decide on the steps that you will take, and then make sure that you know when you are going to take them. Find a calendar, and then use a vision board to ensure that everything is visual and focused. These instruments help to keep your plan top of mind.

The one thing you should not do is become discouraged. This is a big thing you are planning to do, and you'll need to take small steps at first. When you are making massive changes in your lifestyle, you have to accept that some setbacks will occur. Don't allow those setbacks to push you back too much. They are there to help you make progress in the long run.

The most important thing to keep in mind is that you are effectively trying to do your part to save the planet. This kind of thing only ever happens when you take small steps and make sure that each thing you do is from the heart and shows real commitment. You will be helping to save the planet with every choice and decision you make.

Frank Randall

CONCLUSION

I hope this book has given you an insight into sustainability, and helped you make up your mind as to how you can make a valuable difference to the world in your daily life.

As I have done my best to summarize in this small book, it's easy to start out on your journey to self sufficiency. It is always rewarding and will be a beneficial influence to you, your family, home and the environment.

Best wishes,

Frank Randall

Frank Randall

SHOPPING LIST

I've gathered together a shopping list of essential items for a sustainable lifestyle that are available online here:

www.backyardfarmbooks.com/sl

ABOUT THE AUTHOR

Frank was born and bred in Bradford, West Yorkshire, England, in 1945. Born into a family of mill workers, he spent much of his free time on the Yorkshire Moors feeding his fascination with wildlife and nature. He later went on to lecture at the BICC. In 1995 he immigrated to the USA and now lives in peace on the shores of Lake Erie, Ohio, with his wife, two dogs, a colony of honeybees, and a menagerie of other critters.

He's the author of Amazon's #1 Best Selling Backyard Farm Books, which include *The Bee Book for Beginners*, *The Worm Book for Beginners*, and *The Mushroom Book for Beginners* and *The Sustainable Living Book for Beginners*.

@BackyardFarmBks
facebook.com/BackyardFarmBooks
backyardfarmbooks.com

Frank Randall

YOUR FREE GIFT

To get your FREE copy of '**Organic Gardening**' just visit…

www.backyardfarmbooks.com/og

…and sign up for my free newsletter.

If you have a minute to leave a review of '**The Sustainable Living Book for Beginners**' at Amazon that would be fantastic!

This URL will take you straight to the review page:

www.backyardfarmbooks.com/srev

Many thanks.

Frank Randall

ALSO FROM THIS AUTHOR

Frank Randall

The Sustainable Living Book for Beginners

ALSO FROM THIS AUTHOR

Frank Randall

The Sustainable Living Book for Beginners

ALSO FROM THIS AUTHOR

CPSIA information can be obtained at www.ICGtesting.com
Printed in the USA
LVOW10s1313051016

507223LV00003B/425/P